My favorite sounds
from A to Z /

MY FAVORITE Sounds FROM A to Z

Written by **Peggy Snow**

Illustrated by **Brian Barber**

Maren Green Publishing, Inc.

Oak Park Heights, Minnesota

For Greta. — P.S.

~

For Wyatt and Aden. — B.B.

Ages 3 and up

Maren Green Publishing, Inc.
5525 Memorial Avenue North, Suite 6
Oak Park Heights, MN 55082
Toll-free 800-287-1512

Text copyright © 2007 Peggy Snow
Illustrations © 2007 Brian Barber

Library of Congress Control Number: 2007926550

Edited by Pamela Espeland
Text set in Baskerville
Illustrations created digitally

First Edition June 2007
10 9 8 7 6 5 4 3 2 1
Manufactured in China

ISBN: 978-1-934277-02-7

www.marengreen.com

A a

Acorns Cracking

The oak tree spreads its branches over the sidewalk.
Acorns fall with a plop.
I hear the acorns cracking until my bicycle comes to a stop.
My feet touch the ground. *Scrunch!*
Soon, squirrels will feast on their lunch.

B b

Babbling Brook

A babbling brook flows past my house.
It gurgles as it runs through the woods
Toward the clear blue lake.
I touch the cool water as it trickles over the rocks,
Then throw in a stick for the current to take.

C c

Crackling Fire

I sit by the crackling fire on a snowy night.
Orange and blue flames dance around the wood.
I hear the fire snap and pop.
Let's roast marshmallows on a stick,
Then put them between crackers with chocolate on top.

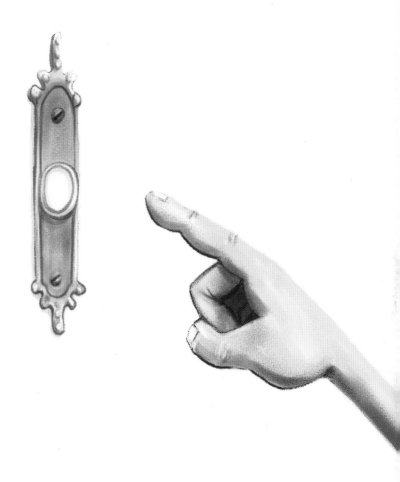

D d

Doorbell Ringing

A doorbell ringing means company is here.
The *ding-dong* tells me
That my friend has come to play.
I go to the door to welcome her.
What will we do today?

E e

Echoing Tunnel

An echoing tunnel leads to my school.
I ride my skateboard through and shout "Hello!"
The tunnel answers "O-o-o-o!"
Sometimes I stop in the middle and sing
To hear the notes repeat and ring.

F f

Flapping Wings

I hear flapping wings overhead.
Geese have come to drink in the pond.
They honk and splash,
Then rise and fly
Soaring high into the sky.

G g

Gravel Crunching

The air is calm, the sky is clear.
Gravel crunching beneath my feet is all I hear
As I walk to collect the mail.
Crunch, crunch, crunch
Comes the sound from each step on the trail.

H h

Horses Galloping

I watch horses galloping across the field.
Their hooves beat the earth like a drum.
They stop to eat apples that have fallen from a tree.
Tails swishing, now they are done.
They turn for home and begin to run.

I i

Icicles Snapping

Long fingers of ice hang from the eaves.
I move my hand across the points
And hear the icicles snapping.
They break and fall,
Now short and small.

Jj

Jingling Bells

Each winter, for a special treat
We go for a ride in a horse-drawn sleigh.
Cuddled under blankets on bales of hay
We hear the horses' jingling bells
And sing carols all the way.

K k

Kites Swooshing

My eyes look to the sky as I hear
Kites swooshing high in the air.
Diamonds, boxes, and pyramids rise,
Then dive and swoop.
Bright tails flapping, they loop the loop.

L l

Laughing Children

At the playground, I see happy faces.
Laughing children take their places.
Joining hands, they make a circle.
Ring around the rosy, we all fall down.
Giggling kids tumble to the ground.

M m

Munching Snacks

Munching snacks sounds good to me.
Crunching apples, chomping carrots,
Nibbling a celery stick or two.
Spread on peanut butter. Dip in dressing.
Munch, crunch, chew.

N n

Nighttime Chirping

I listen to the nighttime chirping of the crickets
In summer, when I go to bed,
The window open near my head.
Fireflies flash by,
Tiny lights in the sky.

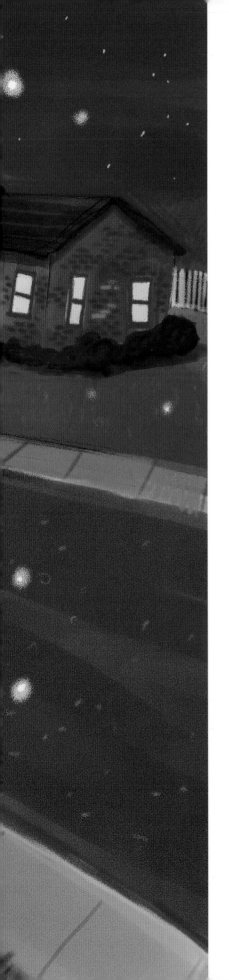

O o

Omelet Sizzling

The eggs have been cracked and whisked in the bowl.
We pour them into the heated pan.
Ssssss is the sound of the omelet sizzling.
Add some ham and grated cheese.
Put it on a plate and pass it, please!

P p
Popping Corn

First, one pop. Then two, then three and four.

Then all I hear is popping corn.

It's pushing the lid off the top of the pan

And popping out onto the floor!

We'll fill our bowls, then make some more.

Q q

Quacking Ducks

The rain has stopped and the clouds have gone away.
Quacking ducks waddle through the sunlit puddles,
Wagging their tail feathers as they walk.
I wonder if they're trying to talk,
Or if they're laughing as they splash and play.

R r

Rustling Leaves

In autumn, trees turn orange and red.
We rake the rustling leaves into a pile,
Then decide to rest awhile.
Leaves crunch and crackle beneath my head
As I fall back on my colorful bed.

S s

Singing Birds

If I wake up very early, I can hear singing birds.
Each one has its own voice and melody.
I pretend they're singing just for me
And I can understand what they say,
Like "Time to get up!" and "It's a wonderful day!".

T t

Teacups Clattering

I hear teacups clattering in the kitchen.
They make a clinking sound on the tray.
Soon we'll have something warm to drink,
With cookies and biscuits.
Teatime is my favorite time of day.

U u

Umbrellas Popping

Waiting for the bus, I look up at the sky.
Dark gray clouds are piled high.
The wind starts to blow and the air turns cool.
Along with the sound of raindrops plopping
Comes the *click, whoosh, snap!* of umbrellas popping.

Vv

Violins Playing

We take our seats in the concert hall and wait.
Soon the orchestra members walk on stage.
The conductor opens her music and turns a page.
I close my eyes and sit still in my chair
As the sweet, soft sound of violins playing fills the air.

W w

Waves Lapping

Sitting on a blanket at the beach,
I love to hear waves lapping on the shore.
The *shush shush* nearly lulls me to sleep.
The waves cover the sand, then ripple back to sea
Leaving shells for me to find and keep.

X x

Xylophones Pinging

I hear the distant sound of ringing,
Beautiful notes from xylophones pinging.
Here comes the marching band down the street,
Wearing hats with feathers
And polished boots on their feet.

Y y

Yelling Crowd

I know lots of places where I can't be loud.
That's why I love a yelling crowd.
At the football field or ballpark, I can be
As noisy as I want to be.
Not like school or the library!

Z z

Zippers Zipping

Camping in the woods brings the sound of zippers zipping.
We set up our tent and zip it shut.
We unzip our sleeping bags, jump inside,
Zip them back up and turn out the light.
Then the zippers are quiet and so are we, snuggled in for the night.

Zzzzzzz.